THE QUINTESSENCE OF THE UPANISHAD

Sri Swami Chidananda

Published by

THE DIVINE LIFE SOCIETY
P.O. SHIVANANDANAGAR—249 192
Distt. Tehri-Garhwal, Uttarakhand, Himalayas, India

Price]   **2007**   [Rs. 30/-

First Edition: 2007
[1,000 Copies]

*Released on the Auspicious and Happy 91st Birthday
Anniversary of H.H. Sri Swami Chidanandaji Maharaj,
the President of the Divine Life Society,
24 September 2007.*

ISBN 81-7052-218-8

EC2

Published by Swami Vimalananda for
The Divine Life Society, Shivanandanagar, and printed
by him at the Yoga-Vedanta Forest Academy Press,
P.O. Shivanandanagar, Distt. Tehri-Garhwal,
Uttarakhand, Himalayas, India

THE QUINTESSENCE OF
THE UPANISHAD

Publisher's Note

In these commentaries on selected verses from the ten principal Upanishads, the fortunate reader is given the great opportunity to delve deeply into the hidden truths within the sacred *mantras*. With clear, simple and concise language, H.H. Sri Swami Chidanandaji Maharaj gently guides the reader beyond the mere words and concepts to their underlying spiritual force. When the aspirant reads the verses and their commentaries with sincere intent, his heart is uplifted and filled with joy. Such is the power of these ancient, sacred texts. We are very grateful to worshipful Swamiji Maharaj for this gift of sharing of his insights and wisdom.

This book is a transcription of a series of short talks given by Swamiji in 1998, to which have been added excerpts from other of his talks given elsewhere that are appropriate to the development of the themes involved. The English translation of the verses has been taken primarily from other Divine Life Society publications.

The Upanishadic vision is not limited to any one race, creed or religion. It has a universal appeal to all sincere spiritual seekers. May all who read this book be blessed with a deeper understanding of Truth.

THE DIVINE LIFE SOCIETY

Sivananda Ashram
24 September 2007

ॐ

10th October 1941,

Beloved aspirants,

There is no book in the whole world that is so thrilling, Soul-stirring and inspiring as the Upanishad.

The philosophy taught by the Upanishads has been the source of solace for many both in the East and the West.

The Upanishads teach the philosophy of absolute unity. They contain the sublime truths of Vedanta and practical hints and clues which throw much light on the pathway of Self-realisation.

Sivananda

Contents

Dedication

Loving adorations to beloved and
revered Holy Master, Gurudev
Sri Swami Sivanandaji Maharaj,
who again and again in so many ways
tried to awaken us to the awareness
that we ever live, not so much in this world,
but we live in God.

Gurudev Sri Swami Sivananda

Nityam-shuddham nirabhasam
nirakaram niranjanam
nitya-bodham Chidanandam
gurum Brahma namamyaham.

To the Guru,
the pure, eternal Brahman, free from reflection,
beyond all names and forms, taintless,
ever awake as Pure Consciousness and
Everlasting Bliss,
our reverential prostrations and adorations.

Asato-maa sat-gamaya,
Tamaso-maa jyotir-gamaya,
Mrityor-maa amritam gamaya!

Lead us from the unreal to the Real;
Lead us from darkness to Light;
Lead us from death to Immortality.

Brihadaranyaka-upanishad [I.3.28]

THE QUINTESSENCE OF
THE UPANISHADS

Sri Swami Chidanandaji Maharaj

Introduction

Worshipful homage unto the supreme, eternal Reality, the one, absolute, transcendental, cosmic Spirit Divine that shines as an eternal Light beyond all darkness! By virtue of the fact that It is transcendental, absolute, one and non-dual, It is present everywhere, encompassing all by Its infinity. Therefore, all existence is Its own manifestation, as it were, is Its own expression. For there can be no other. May the grace of that Being be upon us all!

Om Paramatmane Namah! Salutations to the illumined seers and sages of the sacred Upanishads, who have blessed all humanity with the priceless, eternal treasures of spiritual knowledge and divine wisdom-experience! My reverential prostrations to the holy *brahma-vidya* gurus of the ancient Vedic era! I bow to the exalted memory of towering personalities, like Sage Yajnavalkya, Maharshi Veda Vyasa, Vasishtha and others of high spiritual stature, who contributed their precious wisdom-teachings to enrich the *jnana-kanda* of the Upanishads for the enlightenment of humanity upon this planet Earth.

Last, but not least, in this unbroken line of *brahma-vidya* gurus, my adorations at the divine lotus feet of Satgurudev Parama Pujya Sri Swami Sivanandaji Maharaj, who was an illumined *brahmanistha*, (ever established in Brahman). Gurudev lived, moved and had his being in that Supreme Reality always; and he adored that Supreme Divinity in and through everything he did. Even the minutest action constituted a supreme, glorious worship of the Divine. If we may use the expression "God-filled," then Gurudev was a God-filled being.

Through his radiant personality, his effulgent countenance and his sparkling eyes, he gave us some little faint glimpse of that great glory in whose experience he was firmly established. He shone with a light that is Divinity.

This direct experience of the Truth, *aparoksha'nubhuti*, which Gurudev constantly experienced, made him completely, transparently innocent and simple. He was a sage of wisdom, – people in and around Rishikesh and Haridwar knew him as a towering Vedantic figure, – but his *svabhava* was childlike. His heart was filled with love for all existence, for all the beings and creatures in this world.

Every moment of his life, every breath he took, was dedicated to the sole purpose of awakening a sleeping and slumbering humanity into an awareness of its true eternal identity, of leading people out of the vale of sorrow, pain and suffering in which they found themselves and, by imparting spiritual knowledge, guiding them into a permanent state of blessedness and peace. May his blessings be upon you all!

From time immemorial, in this sacred land of Bharatavarsha (India), a living stream of spirituality, a living stream of *atma-sakshatkara* (Self-realization) and *aparoksha'nubhuti* (direct experience of the Truth) has been flowing continuously as a silent, unseen, inner current for thousands of years. Our religion is not derived from any prophet, messiah or similar historical personality as its author, but from an ancient collection of transcendental wisdom teachings whose origins are shrouded in antiquity.

Over millennia, illumined souls successively recorded their experiences thereby adding to this precious mine of wisdom that came to be known as the Upanishads. The Sanskrit word *Upanishad* comes from the verb *shad*, to sit, and *upani*, near or beneath; it connotes a sitting near, or at the feet of an illumined spiritual master who is a knower of Brahman.

All of the Upanishads taken together are called the Vedanta, because they comprise the *jnana-kanda*, the wisdom teachings of the ancient *rishis*, which are found in the culminating portion of the Vedas. 'Vedanta' means literally the end portion of the Vedas. The *jnana-kanda* of the Vedas is the record of the transcendental experiences of the ancient *rishis* and about what happens to the seeker when he attains that experience.

The *rishis* (the illumined seers and sages of the bygone Vedic age) plumbed the depths of human thought and scaled the highest supreme pinnacles of spiritual experience. Having attained to *Brahma-jnana* (direct knowledge of Brahman), they made declarations, which are as valid today as they were in those ancient times. India is a unique land where the divinity of man was proclaimed and the realization of divinity was declared to be the goal of human existence.

This is the great legacy you have inherited from the ancient seers and sages of Vedic times – the knowledge that you are immortal beings and the knowledge of the ways and means to attain, in this very life, the direct experience of your eternal, true reality. This knowledge is the very essence, the very life-breath, the very soul and central fact of the great, eternal Vedic vision of life we call the *sanatana vaidika dharma*.

You are not this temporary personality consciousness that you think yourself to be. In reality, you are divine. You are immortal spirit. You are ever in a state beyond birth and death. The Light of Consciousness shines in the center of your being as the very core of your own consciousness. It shines within you as the unaffected witness of all things that take place before It, both within and without.

That Light of Consciousness is the eternal Reality; it is the Light of lights which shines beyond all darkness. It pervades everywhere like the light of the sun pervades this solar system of ours. It indwells all things as their immanent principle just as space is present everywhere. This is your reality. This is the truth of your being.

To directly experience this Reality is to become instantly free. Attaining this, one becomes full, perfect, liberated from all sorrow. One attains fearlessness and freedom, the supernal state of *paramananda* (supreme bliss) and indescribable peace. The whole purpose of the talks presented here is to awaken you to this awareness of your true, eternal identity.

May that great Reality, to which we pay homage every morning, shower grace upon you and manifest Itself as this effulgent wisdom awareness, *jnana-jyoti*. May peace be unto you and the joy of this state of illumination, which is coextensive with *sanatana dharma*, which *is sanatana dharma* (the eternal Truth), ever abide in you.

ॐ

Isavasya-Upanishad
[1]

ॐ ईशा वास्यमिद ्ं सर्व
यत्किं च जगत्यां जगत् ।
तेन त्यक्तेन भुञ्जीथा
मा गृधः कस्य स्विद्धनम् ॥१॥

Om Isa-vasyam-idam sarvam
yat-kincha jagatyaam jagat;
Tena tyaktena bhunjeetha
maa gridhah kasya svid-dhanam. [1]

℘

Chapter One

The Hidden One Behind The Many

Commentary

Upanishads are many. Of the numerous Upanishads, 108 are supposed to be the important Upanishads. Of these 108, ten Upanishads are regarded by the scholars and philosophers of our tradition as being the most important because they contain the key that unlocks the quintessence of the transcendental wisdom of all the Upanishads. They are called the "*dasha upanishads.*" Of these ten Upanishads, the Isavasya comes first. The very first *shloka* of this first of the Upanishads says:

All this – whatsoever moves (or moves not) in this universe is indwelt by the Lord. Therefore, by renunciation of the transient, find joy in the Eternal. Do not covet what belongs to others.

Isavasya-upanishad [1]

The central teaching of all Upanishads is that there exists only one, supreme, transcendental Reality, the great, universal, cosmic Spirit Divine, beginningless and endless, eternal, limitless and boundless, immeasurable, vast, beyond time and space, infinite. This Great

Spirit is the absolute, transcendental, non-dual Reality. There exists nothing else besides this.

Therefore, whatever is seen as the many is, verily, that one non-dual Reality manifesting itself in a variety of names and forms. The names and forms may keep changing and, being temporary and transitory, may also disappear. But the origin, substratum, support and ultimate end of all existence never varies. It is the unchanging Reality behind and beyond the ever-changing names and forms that go to make up the universe, which man cognizes through his five senses of perception.

It is the colour in the rainbow and the softness in butter. It is the coldness in the Himalayan snow and the heat of the burning fire. It is the fragrance in jasmine and the coolness in sandal paste. It is the sweetness in honey and the melody in music. It is the wisdom of the sage and the learning of the scholar. It is the whiteness of milk and the salty taste of salt. It pervades all existence, all creation. All things are what they are because that Supreme Reality exists in them as the very essence of their being.

This is the vision that is revealed in the great opening *shloka* of the Isavasya-upanishad: *Isa-vasyam-idam sarvam,* – This entire creation, this entire universe is God-filled. Life is in God, and God is in every part of life. The greatness and grandeur of the Isavasya upanishad lies in this central revelation. Everything else is commentary.

If this truth is to gradually fructify into an experience, if it is to become the basis of our inner conscious-

ness, then it should be practised. That is why Gurudev
Sri Swami Sivananda put this idea into three lines of his
well known Universal Prayer: "Let us behold Thee in all
these names and forms. Let us serve Thee in all these
names and forms. Let us abide in Thee for ever and
ever." He wished for us to recite this every day so as to
freshly evoke within us the awareness of His presence
within and without.

This should be reflected upon and made the basis
of your sight and hearing. Try to behold the one Divine
Principle, the one Divinity hidden in all things, concealed in all things. "Whatever I perceive, whatever I
see, hear, taste, touch and smell is Brahman, the very
goal which I'm trying to attain through my *sadhana*, my
yoga-*abhyasa*, my *japa*, meditation and philosophy.
Daily I perceive that which I am striving for. I live in it. I
move in it. I have my being in it. It is everywhere around
me. That very Being is all around me. He is now, here,
within, without, in all things. This entire universe is
God-filled!"

If this entire universe is God-filled, are we not also
Isvaramaya, God-filled? If God pervades this universe,
does He not pervade you? Is it not a logical conclusion?

You are also God-filled. Deeply ponder this. If
only you absorb this, reflect upon it and keep the
Isavasya-upanishad vision in your heart and mind
always, it will help you to become God-filled. This is
the vital importance of the Isavasya-upanishad and why
this *shloka* was placed at the very beginning.

This then is what we should receive and keep in our hearts. This feeling, this spiritual *bhava*, should be kept up. On the basis of this truth we must try to live. Until your *bhava* penetrates the outer appearance and tries to embrace the concealed, hidden Reality, your senses will perceive only the outer name and form. That's all they will be capable of. It is only *bhava* that penetrates and goes into the heart of the matter.

When *bhava* comes into your life as a permanent factor in the careful attitude you cultivate towards everything you encounter from morning till evening, something happens and things stand before you in a different light. Then this *bhava* will take you into a level beyond the mind and you will realize the Reality, not just as a logical conclusion arrived at through rational processes, but as really real. Intense *bhava* alone has the power ultimately to take you beyond the mind into another level of consciousness, another dimension of consciousness.

The Isavasya-upanishad tells us: "O man! Try to behold the hidden One beyond the visible, superficial many. To be centered in that One is your ultimate goal. By realizing this alone, the mortal becomes immortal. By realizing this alone, the individual soul making this earth journey called life goes beyond all the pain and sorrow, the conflicts and clashes, the envies and jealousies of this terrestrial life and enters into an experience of absolute, indescribable bliss, *sarva dukha nivritti, paramananda prapti*, freedom from all sorrow and attainment of eternal bliss.

This is the covetable state to be attained – sorrowless, full of bliss, fearless and free. Attain this and forever crown your life with glory and become blessed. This is the one thing needful. Thus says the Upanishad.

ॐ

Upanishad.

Kena-Upanishad

[I.1-8]

ॐ केनेषितं पतति प्रेषितं मनः
केन प्राणः प्रथमः प्रैति युक्तः।
केनेषितां वाचमिमां वदन्ति
चक्षुः श्रोत्रं क उ देवो युनक्ति ॥१.१॥

*Om keneshitam patati preshitam manah
kena praanah prathamah praiti yuktah;
keneshitaam vaachamimaam vadanti
chakshuh shrotram ka u devo yunakti.* [I.1]

श्रोत्रस्य श्रोत्रं मनसो मनो य-
द्वाचो ह वाच ꣳ स उ प्राणस्य प्राणः।
चक्षुषश्चक्षुरतिमुच्य धीराः
प्रेत्यास्माल्लोकादमृता भवन्ति ॥१.२॥

*Shrotrasya shrotram manaso mano yad-
vaacho ha vaacham sa u praanasya praanah;
chakshushah-chakshur-atimuchya dheeraah
pretya asmaa-lokaad-amritaa bhavanti.* [I.2]

न तत्र चक्षुर्गच्छति
न वागच्छति नो मनः।
न विद्मो न विजानीमो
यथैतदनुशिष्यात्।
अन्यदेव तद्विदिता-
दथो अविदितादधि।
इति शुश्रुम पूर्वेषां
ये नस्तद्व्याचचक्षिरे ॥१.३॥

Na tatra chakshur-gacchati
na vaak-gacchati no manah;
na vidmo na vijaaneemo
yathetad-anushishyaat.
anyad-eva tat-viditaat-
atho aviditaat-adhi;
iti shushruma purveshaam
ye nastad-vyaachachakshire. [I.3]

यद्वाचानभ्युदितं
येन वागभ्युद्यते।
तदेव ब्रह्म त्वं विद्धि
नेदं यदिदमुपासते ॥१.४॥

Yat-vaacha anabhyuditam
yena vaag-abhyudyate;
Tadeva brahma tvam viddhi
nedam yadida-mupaasate. [I.4]

यन्मनसा न मनुते
येनाहुर्मनो मतम्।
तदेव ब्रह्म त्वं विद्धि
नेदं यदिदमुपासते ॥१.५॥

Yan-manasaa na manute
yenaahu-mano matam;
Tadeva brahma tvam viddhi
nedam yadida-mupaasate. [I.5]

यच्चक्षुषा न पश्यति
येन चक्षूँ षि पश्यति।
तदेव ब्रह्म त्वं विद्धि
नेदं यदिदमुपासते ॥१.६॥

Yat-chakshushaa na pashyati
yena chakshumshi pashyati;
Tadeva brahma tvam viddhi
nedam yadida-mupaasate. [I.6]

यच्छ्रोत्रेण न शृणोति
येन श्रोत्रमिद ँ श्रुतम् ।
तदेव ब्रह्म त्वं विद्धि
नेदं यदिदमुपासते ॥१.७॥

Yat-shrotrena na shrunoti
yena shrotram-idam shrutam;
Tadeva brahma tvam viddhi
nedam yadida-mupaasate. [I.7]

यत्प्राणेन न प्राणिति
येन प्राणः प्रणीयते।
तदेव ब्रह्म त्वं विद्धि
नेदं यदिदमुपासते ॥१.८॥

Yat-praanena na praaniti
yena praanah praneeyate;
Tadeva brahma tvam viddhi
nedam yadida-mupaasate. [I.8]

༺

Chapter Two

Consciousness Alone Perceives Consciousness

Disciple: *Who impels the mind to alight on its objects? At whose command does life first proceed to function? Who impels us to utter these words? What intelligence (or divine power) directs the eyes and the ears (towards their respective objects)?* (I.1)

Preceptor: *It is the Ear of the ear, the Mind of the mind, the Tongue of the Tongue (the Speech of the Speech), the Life of the life and Eye of the eye. Having abandoned (the sense of self or I-ness in these) and rising above sense-life, the wise become immortal.* (I.2)

The eye does not go there, nor speech, nor the mind. We do not, therefore, know how to instruct one about it. It is different from what is known and it is beyond what is unknown. Thus, we have heard from the ancient preceptors who taught us. (I.3)

That which is not expressible through speech but That by which speech is expressed know That alone as Brahman, and not this which people worship here. (I.4)

What one cannot think with the mind, but by which they say that the mind is made to think, know That alone as Brahman, and not this which people worship here. (I.5)

What cannot be seen by the eye, but by which the eyes are able to see, know That alone as Brahman, and not this which people worship here. (I.6)

What cannot be heard by the ear, but by which the ears are able to hear, know That alone as Brahman and not this which people worship here. (I.7)

What cannot be indrawn with breath, but That whereby breath is indrawn, know that alone to be Brahman, and not what people here adore. (I.8)

Kena-upanishad [I.1-8]

Commentary

That alone is Brahman, the supreme transcendental Reality, which does not require the mind to know or cognize anything, for it is itself the Knower of all things known. It is the Seer of all things. The mind is but a finite instrument, limited in time and space, evolved or created out of that supreme Reality. The finite can never know the Infinite. The limited can never know the Unlimited; rather, it is Brahman that is the supreme Knower of the mind.

Mind cognizes dimly, as through a mist, only the temporary manifestations and expressions of that supreme, unmanifest, transcendental Reality. Yet, people think they have known Brahman by only a little study, by a little bit of empirical knowledge, by a merely rational, intellectual grasp of these ideas. This is not the kind of knowledge that can liberate.

What people worship as God, as Bhagavan, as the supreme Reality, verily, verily, is not the true Reality. The Reality is beyond the grasp of the mind and the perceptive power of the senses. Neither through the senses can it be perceived, nor through the mind can it be thought of, nor through logic and the rational processes of the intellect can it be grasped, for it is the subtlest of the subtle. It is only in the depths of one's awakened and illumined consciousness that it can be experienced.

It is an experience, not an object of perception. It is an experience, not an idea to be grasped by the mind. It is an experience, not something to be attained through reason and logic, for it is Pure Consciousness. And within each individual soul, there is a potential of that essence of Consciousness. That is the Reality within each being. It is the spiritual, innermost core of the human individual, the *svaroopa*, one's real identity, eternal and imperishable.

It is through one's spiritual center, which is of the nature of pure Consciousness, that the supreme Eternal Consciousness, *chidananda svaroopa brahman*, or *chitswaroopa brahman*, or *chinmaya chidghana brahman*, can be grasped. Consciousness alone can perceive Consciousness. Therefore, what is felt here or what is regarded here as God, is not the ultimate Divine Reality. Brahman is that which transcends body, senses, mind, intellect and all inner processes. It transcends everything. That is to be known. That is the Knower of all things known, the Seer of all things seen. When That is

experienced through Consciousness, one becomes liberated. This is the truth. This, therefore, is the way.

ॐ

Katha-Upanishad
[I.3.14]

उत्तिष्ठत जाग्रत
प्राप्य वरान्निबोधत।
क्षुरस्य धारा निशिता दुरत्यया
दुर्गं पथस्तत्कवयो वदन्ति ॥१.३.१४॥

Uttishthata jaagrata
praapya varaan nibodhata;
Kshurasya dhaaraa nishitaa duratyayaa
durgam pathastat kavayo vadanti. [I.3.14]

ॐ

Chapter Three

The Immortality of the Soul

Arise! Awake! Having reached the great (teachers), learn (realize that Atman). Like the sharp edge of a razor is that path, difficult to cross and hard to tread, – thus, the wise say.

Katha-upanishad [I.3.14]

Commentary

"Arise! Awake! Approaching those wise men of illumination and enlightenment, know the great Reality and become enlightened!" This is the stirring call of the Upanishads sounded long ago in the hoary age of the Vedas in this great land of *avataras*, in this great land of enlightened sages, seers and illumined masters who had attained liberation and God-experience. This call is not confined only to the age in which it was sounded. Nor is it confined merely to the fortunate dwellers of Bharatavarsha, the spiritual leader of the entire world. It is an eternal call addressed to all human beings on earth beyond all limits of either country or nationality or religion or philosophy.

All human beings are called upon to awaken and realize that theirs is a divine destiny. Their time here on the earth plane is not to be confined to merely gross, material matters, culminating in death. Each individual soul is born here with a divine destiny – to realize one's reality, to realize one's immortal nature, the immortality of the individual soul.

The body may be perishable; it comes and goes. But the body is not the reality. The body is only a little mortal vestment, a temporary medium or channel, as it were, necessary for functioning upon this earth plane. Just as a person discards an old and tattered garment and acquires one that is new, so also the embodied Self casts off a worn-out body and enters another that is new. (Bhagavad Gita II:22.) Of this, the sage has no doubt.

The immortality of the soul is the great message declared by our Upanishadic seers. It is a message for the entire global human family to accept and, thus, become blessed. This call sounded long, long ago from the forest vastness of the Himalayan heights of spiritual India. This is the real Bharatavarsha. Real Bharatavarsha is not the social India, nor the political India, nor the geographical India. The real Bharatavarsha is spiritual India. This is the truth.

This eternal call has resounded through millennia, through the corridor of centuries. Generation after generation, it has been re-echoed in the teachings of Masters of wisdom to their disciples. "Even as this truth has been handed over by me, O my beloved one, you must hand it over in your own generation to the next qualified disciples so that living spirituality will always be present as a dynamic undercurrent of India." Thus, have the disciples been commissioned. Therefore, this call to arise, awake and become illumined by experiencing the supreme Reality is as relevant, important and necessary today as it was when it was declared by our ancients in the hoary past.

Let the world recognize this. Let the world arise, awake, and discard its mere materialism and blind hedonism. Say NO to the pursuit of pleasure as the goal of life. You are made for higher things! Respond to this call and attain blessedness. Realize your immortality and divinity and fulfil the goal of life. Then alone your life is a real success. Thus be it.

ॐ

Prasna-Upanishad
[VI.5-6]

सा यथेमा नद्यः स्यन्दमानाः समुद्रायणाः

समुद्रं प्राप्यास्तं गच्छन्ति भिद्येते

तासां नामरूपे समुद्र इत्येवं प्रोच्यते।

एवमेवास्य परिद्रष्टुरिमाः षोडश कलाः

पुरुषायणाः पुरुषं प्राप्यास्तं गच्छन्ति

भिद्येते चासां नामरूपे पुरुष इत्येवं

प्रोच्यते स एषोऽकलोऽमृतो भवति तदेष

श्लोकः ॥६.५॥

*Sa yathemaa nadyah syandamaanaah samudraa-
yanaah samudram praapyaastam gachhanti bhidyete
taasaam naamarupe samudra ityevam prochyate,
Evamevaasya paridrishtuh-imaah shodashakalaah
purushaayanaah purusham praapyaastam gacchanti
bhidhyete chaasaam naamarupe purusha ityevam
prochyate sa eshah-akalah-amritah bhavati. Tadesha
shlokah* [VI.5]

अरा इव रथनाभौ
कला यस्मिन्प्रतिष्ठिताः ।
तं वेद्यं पुरुषं वेद
यथा मा वो मृत्युः परिव्यथा इति ॥६.६॥

Araa iva rathanaabhau
kalaa yasmin-pratishthitaah;
Tam vedyam purusham veda
yathaa maa vo mrityuh parivyathaa iti. [VI.6]

ॐ

Chapter Four

The Oneness of All

6.5: Just as these rivers flowing towards the sea disappear when they have reached the sea, their names and forms vanishing into what is called 'sea,' so also these sixteen parts[1] of the witness that go towards the Purusha (Supreme Spirit, the Atman-Brahman) disappear, their names and forms merging into Spirit, and all is called Purusha alone.

6.6: Know that Purusha who ought to be known, in whom the kalaas (parts) are centered like spokes in the nave of a wheel, in order that death may not afflict you.

Prasna-upanishad [VI.5-6]

---

1 The sixteen parts or 'kalaas' are listed in vs. VI.4: "He (the Purusha) created prana, from prana, faith, akasa, air, fire, water, earth, senses, mind and food; and from food, strength, penance, mantras, karma and worlds and in the worlds name also." Sri Swami Sivananda writes in his Commentary, "Kalaas are mere appearances. They are not real parts of the Purusha. They are manifestations of His illusory power." "The Purusha has no parts really. It is indivisible, homogeneous and partless. When one attains knowledge, all conditions drop away and one beholds the one homogeneous, unconditioned Supreme Purusha alone."

Commentary

Just as various rivers, which have different names and places of origin and different pathways to the ocean, ultimately lose their distinction when they reach the ocean and become one with it, so, too, do the seekers of Truth, even though following different paths or traditions, ultimately enter the selfsame liberating experience – the ocean of *Satchidananda*, the ocean of the eternal Pure Consciousness, known in the Upanishads as 'Brahman' or the Great Reality.

This great truth, discovered by our ancients, is of utmost importance to our world today, rent as it is by clashes and conflicts between the different religions, each claiming uniqueness and each claiming that theirs is the only authentic way to realize God. They do not know that the Great Reality is one and identical and that all these seemingly different religions are but various pathways towards the same supreme goal. Their origin may be different, the course they follow may be different, but their goal is one. *Ekam sat viprah bahudah vadanti*. (The Reality is one; it is described variously by scholars.) Thus has it been declared in the great Upanishads.

In disregarding this great wisdom teaching from the past, we are doing the very unwise thing of emphasizing differences rather than trying to find the common ground that unifies. Today more than ever, we need harmony, brotherhood, unity and oneness. The world is in great need of this approach to life and this new attitude towards one another, for all human beings belong to one great family under the parenthood of the one, supreme, universal Reality, call it God or Mother or Spirit Divine. It is Father, Mother, Friend, Relative. It is your All-in-all.

Why limit it to human beings? As a matter of fact, not only human beings, but all creatures created by that Supreme Being are related in kinship. Every bird, every beast, every insect, reptile, submarine creature, small and great, all are included. We all belong to one cosmic, spiritual fraternity. This is indeed the vision that is needed today, this approach to life and this attitude concerning all beings.

Our ancients went so far as to say that not only the living and moving creatures, but even the immobile, botanical species, the grass that grows under our feet, the plants, creepers, trees, are also a part of this great universal family. It is said that this one Great Reality slumbers in the stone and mineral, breathes in plants and creepers, moves about in all animals, but thinks, feels and reasons in the crown and glory of all creation, the human species. There is only one Consciousness; its manifestation is of different, varied degrees. This truth has to be recognized.

This Great Reality is the one common consciousness that unites the entire universe and all the living beings in a spiritual unity, just as one single thread holds together all the variegated beads in a necklace. The beads may be of different colors, different shapes, different sizes, but they are all strung on one single, identical thread or *sutra*. It is the one within the many, the identical within the seemingly different. Even so, one common Consciousness, the '*sutra-atman*', is present in all beings, in all people, in all nations, in all countries. Whether it is the American or the Canadian or the people of Europe, India, Pakistan, Sri Lanka, Burma (now Myanmar), Bangladesh, China, Japan, Indonesia – we are all one.

When we look with a little depth, differences vanish. They are merely superficial. And the underlying unity, which is the essence, becomes apparent. If we can look upon one another with this spiritual vision, then all these clashes and conflicts, all the various attitudes which are negative and hostile, will vanish and only unity will remain. Then will be the possibility of the dawn of a new era in which human beings move as one, hold hands together, and engage in shared tasks for the welfare of all.

This is the great vision – an enlightened humanity, a worldwide community in which human beings are educated so as to realize this enlightenment. This vision must be awakened in the minds and hearts of human beings everywhere. Until and unless man's spiritual higher nature is awakened, the world will not change. This is the great need of the hour.

Our educational systems, therefore, are in vital need of a complete transformation. Today, whatever little education one receives is completely career-oriented. It is designed in order to provide personnel for the great industrial and commercial concerns, not for the cultivation of the higher dimensions of the human personality. The products of such educational systems are human beings who are totally enslaved by their lower propensities and societies in which the whole lifestyle is geared only in order to stoke up and excite more and more passion, greed, sensuality and self-centeredness.

Education should be more than putting into the human brain a great many facts and figures. It is not like feeding statistical data into a computer. On the contrary, the process of true education is a reverse process. It is a positive, creative process designed to draw forth from within the human individual the hidden great qualities of love, unity, harmony, brotherhood and peace. Such individuals will then be able to raise the level of contemporary social life and enrich the social life stream, its beauty, virtue and goodness.

Therefore, an important goal of education should be to impart to the child an awareness of its higher spiritual nature. Then the child will begin to feel, "I am not separate from anyone else. Everyone is my own self, my own reflection. So I must have the same attitude towards others as I have towards myself. Just as I want the best for myself, I must try to bring about the best for all." Then alone education will have some sense. Otherwise, the educational process is just the filling in of information from outside and leaving the inner spirit completely slumbering and unawakened.

If just a little of this spiritual dimension could become part of our educational process, then indeed the Twenty-first Century would soon be an era of oneness, harmony, real brotherhood, human welfare, peace and prosperity for one and all. Thus, this Upanishad gives us the key to the ultimate state of unity towards which all of us must sincerely and earnestly work so that our tomorrow will be a golden tomorrow.

ॐ

Mundaka-Upanishad

[III.2.2,4]

कामान्यः कामयते मन्यमानः
स कामभिर्जायते तत्र तत्र।
पर्याप्तकामस्य कृतात्मनस्तु
इहैव सर्वे प्रविलीयन्ति कामाः ॥३.२.२॥

*Kaamaanyah kaamayate manyamaanah
sa kaamabhir-jaayate tatra tatra;
Paryaapta-kaamasya krit-aatmana-stu
ihaiva sarve pravileeyanti kaamaah. [III.2.2]*

नायमात्मा बलहीनेन लभ्यो
न च प्रमादात्तपसो वाप्यलिङ्गात् ।
एतैरुपायैर्यतते यस्तु विद्वांस्तस्यैष
आत्मा विशते ब्रह्म धाम ॥३.२.४॥

*Naayam-aatmaa balaheenena labhyo
na cha pramaadaat-tapaso vaapy-alingaat;
Etaih-upaayaih-yatate yastu vidvaamtasya-esha
aatmaa vishate brahma-dhaama. [III.2.4]*

Chapter Five

Be The Master of Your Body-House

He who forms desires in his mind is born again here and there through his longing for objects of desire. But he who has reached the Goal of all longing, whose soul has found fulfilment, all his desires vanish even here on earth.

Mundaka-upanishad [III.2.2]

The Self (Atman) cannot be realized by one who is destitute of strength or without earnestness or by penance without 'mark'.[2] But the wise who strive in the right way lead their soul into the supreme abode of Brahman.

Mundaka-upanishad [III.2.4]

---

2 Gurudev Sri Swami Sivananda gives two interpretations for the phrase "by penance without 'mark.'" The first refers to one who practices extreme austerities such as torturing the body, etc.; the other interpretation refers to those without the 'mark' of authorized Sannyasa, renunciation.

Commentary

Attaining that supreme abode of *Brahma-jnana* (the direct knowledge of Brahman), *yat gatva na nivartante tat dhaama parmam mama*, one does not come back again into this world of birth and death characterized by *janma, mrityu, jara, vyadhi, dukha* – birth, death, old age, disease and sorrow. One becomes liberated from the ever-recurring wheel of transmigration, *punarapi jananam punarapi maranam, punarapi janani jathare shayanam* – to be born again, to die again, and again to suffer in the mother's womb. Attaining that supreme state of Self-knowledge, one becomes immortal.

Our ancients attained this wondrous state of blessedness. Not wishing to keep the method of their success a secret for themselves alone, but determined to share it with all sincere seeking souls, they issued a great call: Come! Be strong! Be determined! What we have achieved, you can also achieve! Having attained the greatest gift of God, the gift of human status, do not miss this golden opportunity!

Listen to what we say! Until one has conquered the desire for sense enjoyment, the truth will not shine in him. So long as these vain desires of your senses are clamoring and, as it were, dragging you outwards every moment, making you a slave to everything outside – to a little colour, a little taste, a little touch – notwithstanding all your pretensions, how can the truth express itself in your heart?

Perfection is one thing and enjoyment another; these two having different ends, engage people differently. A thoughtless person, deluded by the folly of riches and sensual pleasures, never stops to consider these truths. 'This world exists, the other does not,' thinking thus they come again and again under the power of death.

Therefore be strong! "If you are seeking liberation, my child, shun the objects of the senses like poison! And seek forgiveness, sincerity, kindness, contentment and truth like you would seek nectar." (Ashtavakra Gita-2.)

The Atman cannot be attained by the weak! The weak and vacillating are easily dragged by their senses into the pursuit of pleasures. They are enslaved by their desires and waste away their lives trying to fulfill this never-ending fire of desire. Know this truth: desires can never be fulfilled! They are endless; they keep on multiplying. If you pour an oblation onto a blazing fire, do you think the fire will receive it, become satisfied and then subside? On the contrary, it will burn with redoubled vigour. Desire is like that fire.

"The deer, black-bee, moth, elephant, and fish — each one of these meets with its death because of its attachment to one or the other of its five sense-organs. The ignorant man is attached to all his five senses! How can he ever find happiness in this world!" (Yoga Vasishtha.)

Therefore, be determined! Reject desire! Prove yourself to be the master of your body-house. Don't be a slave in your own house. Manifest your strength! Then alone will you be able to attain the Atman. With leonine determination, turn away from the allurement of sense objects, from the temptation of desires. Direct all your energy (physical, mental and *pranic* energies) towards meditation and yogic *sadhana*, and in this way attain the goal of life!

Think resolutely: A golden opportunity has been given to me. I am not going to be stupid enough to miss it! I shall be wise! I shall not allow anything to divert me from this path. As an arrow shot from a bow wings its way straight to the target, thus shall be my life and thus shall I attain victory! I shall succeed in this quest and forever become blessed!

ॐ

Taittiriya-Upanishad

[II.9]

यतो वाचो निवर्तन्ते।
अप्राप्य मनसा सह।
आनन्दं ब्रह्मणो विद्वान् ।
न बिभेति कुतश्चनेति ॥२.९॥

Yato vaacho nivartante,
apraapya manasaa sah.
Aanandam brahmano vidvaan,
na bibheti kutashchaneti. [II.9]

ॐ

Chapter Six

The Common Desire for Peace and Happiness

He who knows the bliss of Brahman from which all words return without reaching it, together with the mind, is not afraid of anything....

Taittiriya-Upanishad [II.9]

Commentary

In this human world, there is one thing that is common to all human beings, no matter how different may be the external nature of their lives. Their food, clothing, appearance, language, customs and traditions, everything may be different, but one thing is common. What is that common factor? No one wants to suffer pain or sorrow. You can ask anyone, "Do you wish to be in pain?" Everyone will say, "No!" And no one likes to be oppressed by any type of fear. Fear is something that is perceived as a great oppressing force. Everyone wants happiness, joy and bliss. Everyone wants to be fearless. These are common factors among all human beings.

Is such attainment possible in today's world where there are so many causes for fear, anxiety, worry, and even dread? Where terrorism, unfortunately, is on the rise and large sectors of mankind seem overcome with a dire, impelling desire to kill, destroy and wreak havoc? In such a world, is it possible to become fearless and free and, at the same time, to have supreme bliss?

Yes. The *shloka* says that beyond the grasp of mind and speech (which means that human language cannot describe it), there exists a Great Reality. If that Great Reality is realized, one instantly becomes fearless and free, one becomes sorrowless and filled with bliss. Who will not want it? Everyone is seeking only this! God did not send us here to suffer and fear, to weep and wail. No! God's plan for human beings is to reach a state of fear-lessness and supreme bliss and joy. Knowing this, let us cooperate with His wonderful plan and wisely do all that is needful to attain that supreme state by making this human vehicle an instrument of devotion, *sadhana*, and yogic *abhyasa* (practice)

Just as a mirror covered with thick, black, sticky smoke has to be cleaned a number of times to make it completely pure and capable of giving a clear reflection, similarly, the mirror of our mind, which is Conscious-ness-Bliss in its original state, is covered by the smoke of ignorance and desire. It is these that are removed in successive stages by dedicated *sadhana*.

Although we say, after each cleaning, that the mir-ror is becoming more and more clear, it is important to remember that the mirror by itself is *always* clean and capable of clear reflection. It is the smoke or the dirt, which covered it, that is removed in stages every time it is cleaned.

Similarly, in your innermost spiritual consciousness, you are ever a shining center of peace and joy. You are full of purity, full of love, full of compassion, full of harmony, full of unity, full of light. You are *jyotishaam-api taj jyotis-tamasah paramuchyate.* (You are the Light of lights beyond all darkness). (Bhagavad Gita XIII.17.) And you are unutterable Bliss. Those who have experienced this highest state have declared, "Brahman prevails as Bliss and Bliss alone." You are ever rooted in this Bliss. You ever abide in this Bliss. In your true essential being, as a spiritual essence, you ever abide in this Bliss.

To try to become aware of your real identity, of the inner center of your being, is the essence of *sadhana* (spiritual practice). For from that awareness only can you unfold your divine identity. God is nearer to you than the nearest object in this universe. He is nearer to you than your life's breath, nearer than your hands and feet. He is the very Self of your being, the very basis of your being.

When a beautiful, long-stemmed flower is put in a tall vase filled with water, not only does the vase support it and keep it upright, but the life-giving water sustains its life and keeps it fresh and blooming. In the same way every creature on earth, every form of life, derives its life from God who upholds it. Because it is in God, it also lives in God, for God is life.

God is the source of all life. If you are alive, it is because of His living presence within which is life itself. He is *Satchidananda* (Existence-Consciousness-Bliss

Absolute). He is Existence; therefore, you exist. You think, feel, move and are vitally alive because He is within you as *chit*, as luminous Consciousness. If only you can maintain the purity of this inner essence of your being, learn to live continuously in its awareness and learn to keep a continuous stream of this awareness as your life's breath, then you will find that you also abide in Bliss.

All other experiences are merely relative, existing in the plane of phenomenality and duality. All other experiences pertain to the dimension of the intellect, mind and body, to the plane of the physical and psychological, which is always subject to change. This is a world of transience, a world of the ever-changing pairs of opposites – sweet and bitter, pleasure and pain, joy and sorrow. But the essence of your being has nothing to do with this dimension of phenomenality, for it is not in the relative plane of time and space. That is why the *shloka* says, "*All words return without reaching It, together with the mind.*" The physical and psychological experiences cannot reach It. That state of Being is pure bliss. It is pure peace and joy in which you are free and fearless. "*He who knows the bliss of Brahman ... is no more afraid of anything.*"

Therefore, let us be wise! Let us make use of this life for the attainment of this supreme destiny. Becoming filled with bliss, let us become truly fearless forever!

Mandukya-Upanishad

[7]

नान्तःप्रज्ञं नबहिःप्रज्ञं नोभयतःप्रज्ञं
नप्रज्ञानघनं नप्रज्ञं नाप्रज्ञम् । अदृश्यम-
व्यवहार्यमग्राह्यमलक्षणमचिन्त्यमव्यपदे-
श्यमेकात्मप्रत्ययसारं प्रपञ्चोपशमं
शान्तं शिवमद्वैतं चतुर्थं मन्यन्ते
स आत्मा स विज्ञेयः ॥७॥

*Na-antah-prajnam, na-bahih-prajnam, na-ubhayatah-
prajnam, na-prajnaana-ghanam, na-prjnam, na-
aprajnam, adrishyam-avyavahaaryam-agraahyam-
alakshanam-achintyam-avyapade-shyam-eka-atma-
pratyaya-saaram, prapanchopashamam, shaantam,
shivam-advaitam, chaturtham manyante, sa aatmaa
sa vijneyah.* [7]

ॐ

Chapter Seven

Beyond the Three States of Consciousness

The wise think that the fourth (state), the Turiya, is not that which is conscious of the internal (subjective) world, nor that which is conscious of the external (objective) world, nor that which is conscious of both, nor that which is a compact mass of knowledge, nor that which is simple consciousness, nor that which is insentient.

It is unseen, unrelated, incomprehensible, indefinable, unthinkable, indescribable, the sole essence of the consciousness of the Self with no trace of the phenomenal world, the peaceful, the auspicious, and the non-dual. This is the Atman, the Self and it is to be realized.

Mandukya-upanishad [7]

Commentary

The Supreme Reality is incomprehensible and indescribable. It is neither consciousness, nor unconsciousness, nor that which is perceived, nor that which perceives. As such, all efforts of the human individual to attain knowledge of it through the senses and the mind, the two faculties with which man is endowed for knowing the world around him, are bound to be futile.

"All speech, together with the mind, return without reaching it. *Yato vacho nivartante apraapya manasaa sah.*" (Taittiriya II.9.) 'All speech' means *all* the senses, the senses of sight, hearing, taste, touch and smell. These senses, together with the mind that observes, compares, contrasts, understands and grasps the meaning of what is perceived, are our faculties for obtaining knowledge. As all the objects of the world are outside one's being, these faculties have an outgoing tendency, from within to without. They project outwards in order to cognize the external, outside world.

But the Supreme Reality cannot be known by these faculties, for the simple reason that the created cannot comprehend that which existed before itself. The Supreme Reality existed when nothing else existed. It is the Creator of all things created, the one, supreme, causeless cause of all that exists; yet, it is itself without any cause because it has ever existed. It is the Eternal Reality. Therefore, the Supreme Reality cannot come within the range of human perception and cognition, and any attempt to obtain knowledge of it through the senses and the mind is bound to be fruitless and futile.

Then, can it be known at all? "Yes and no" is the answer. Although it can never be known by your senses and mind, you are something more than the five senses and the mind. You are beyond all categories and faculties. The *siddhanta* (the established doctrine) says you are "*sharira traya vilakshana, pancha kosha ateeta, avastha traya saakshee"*. You are beyond the five sheaths of which the human individual is composed, and you are beyond the three states of consciousness (waking, dreaming and deep sleep) that the human individual experiences everyday. You are the witness of these three states.

The first sheath, *annamaya kosha,* is the sheath of food identical with the physical body. The second sheath, *pranamaya kosha,* is the sheath of *prana,* or vital energy. Then there is the sheath of the mind and the sheath of the intellect, *manomaya kosha* and *vijnanamaya kosha,* which are in the subtle body. The fifth sheath is the sheath of bliss, *anandamaya kosha*, which is located in the causal body. But you are '*pancha kosha ateeta*'. You are that which transcends the five sheaths.

Similarly, you are beyond the three states of consciousness through which the *atman* moves, as though, during each cycle of twenty-four hours. The waking world is seen during the waking state. With the senses and the mind, you are able to hear sounds, to see things. A second world is created by the mind subjectively while you are dreaming which you cognize as though it is real.

The dream experience is so graphic and so complete in all respects and dominates your consciousness so completely that, during that period, it remains the only truth for you. You can perceive and experience every detail of the dream through all your five sense-organs. But when you wake up suddenly due to the ringing of the alarm clock, the very next moment everything disappears, everything becomes unreal and you say, "It was only a dream."

Our seers say that this waking world is just like a dream, that everything perceived through the five senses and understood by the mind and the intellect is unreal. All the objects of the world are like the water of a desert mirage or the glint of silver in the mother-of-pearl lying on the sand of the seashore. They have no real existence, but only a seeming and temporary appearance. When you wake up to the supreme, cosmic Reality, your true identity, then you will know that your present identity was as much a figment of your imagination as the characters and all the factors in your last night's dream.

And during deep sleep (sleep without dream) even though you are not aware of any universe at that time, you are aware, upon awakening, that you have passed through a state of calm, restful, peaceful, refreshing sleep. In the morning when you wake up, should someone ask you if you slept well, you can clearly affirm, "Yes, yes, I enjoyed a sound, restful sleep." This, itself, shows that you are the *experiencer* of these three states and not something identified with the states. 'You' are the unchanging Reality that transcends the three states.

According to the Vedanta, anything coming within the range of the waking, dreaming and deep sleep states cannot be considered as comprising the Reality. Vedanta gives a specific definition for Reality. What is truly, authentically and genuinely Real? You have to try to understand with a very subtle intellect what Vedanta wants to convey to you.

That alone can be called '*Sat*', authentically and genuinely Real, which is beginningless and endless, which is ever present, which ever *is* in all the three periods of time. It always existed in the past, it exists in the present and will always exist in the future as well. It will never cease to be. There is a further qualification: that is the Reality which abides always, in all the three periods of time without undergoing any change. It always remains the same. Nothing can alter it, nothing can change it. It is ever Full, ever Perfect.

This is the specific, classical definition of *Sat*, the Supreme Reality: *Sat* is always present and unchangeable. If you apply this test to anything in this world, you will find that all *things* fail to fulfil this requirement. All *things* change right from the beginning. Your body changes right from birth, so it cannot be the Reality. Your human personality did not exist before you were born and it exists here on this earth plane for a limited time only. And during the dream state, there is another body and another world which appears as one hundred percent true so long as you remain in the dream state, but disappears in a fraction of a second once you return to the waking state. And during deep sleep, all vanishes.

Therefore, anything coming within the range of the waking, dreaming and deep sleep states cannot be considered as comprising the Reality. But the *experiencer* of these three states, which is Pure Consciousness, transcends these. That is to be known. That is the eternal, unchanging Reality. It is regarded as the fourth state, the Turiya.

You exist as the fourth state. You *are*, even now, the absolute Reality, beyond phenomena, beyond birth and death. This knowledge – the direct perception and experience of your eternal, imperishable, divine identity – liberates you forever from all the limitations and imperfections that pertain to your present temporary state of individuality, where you think of yourself as a limited, human individual subject to birth and death, change, old age, and various moods and mental states. You become liberated from all the pains of *samsara*, as it were, and become established in a state of indescribable felicity and supreme joy.

This is the supreme knowledge, *jnana*, which transcends all other knowledge, attaining which one does not come back again into this world of pain and death, knowing which everything else is known. This is the raft that can safely take you across the ocean of *samsara* (worldly existence).

So, meditation on these three states of waking, dream and deep sleep results in the dawn of the knowledge that the Self (the pure, non-dual Consciousness) alone IS. The three states are only the expression of that unborn, eternal, changeless Atman. After hearing this truth (*sravana*) from one's own guru, one should reflect on it (*manana*). The experience of deep sleep and dream gives the clue to conclude that one is the pure, unsullied Consciousness in all the three states, in spite of the appearance and disappearance of a so-called real world, an unreal world, and the absence of the two. Reflection has to be done till all doubts are eliminated root and branch.

The instructions from the guru are themselves not the Truth. They produce ideas in the mind, whereas the Truth is beyond the mind. Still, they help you to reflect and practise deep meditation (*nididhyasana*). Without them, no one can proceed on the spiritual path. The guru and the scriptures are trying to communicate through words that which can never be expressed through words. Hence, one has to hear their instructions with all attention and complete faith and, at the same time, go beyond all words and mental concepts by means of deep meditation.

Ultimately, deep meditation is the one and only *sadhana* that can bring about illumination. However it may be described, ultimately all yogas culminate in meditation because it is in and through such meditation alone that illumination is attained. The word 'meditation' as such may not be used, but it is deep meditation, *nididhyasana*, that is intended.

For example, in the nine modes of devotion of *bhakti* yoga, meditation does not seem to be mentioned, but *atma-nivedanam* (total self-surrender) means nothing but that – becoming a zero, totally losing oneself through concentrated devotion into a state of meditation. It means meditation. In all the yogas, meditation is the ultimate portal or gateway to blessedness.

Therefore, make use of the faculties given to you. Ponder these truths. Direct your mind upwards and attain an experience transcending the three states. Attain an experience of the fourth state, the Turiya, and then you will become liberated. The existence of this fourth state is unknown to the vast majority of people. It was discovered by our ancient sages and seers of Vedic times. It is our great good fortune that they have made clear to us the great goal to be attained, the goal that will liberate the human individual from all pain and sorrow. The Turiya, the fourth state, – this is to be attained.

ॐ

Aitareya-Upanishad

[V.3]

एष ब्रह्मैष इन्द्र एष प्रजापतिरेते सर्वे देवा इमानि च पञ्च
महाभूतानि पृथिवी वायुराकाश आपो ज्योतींषीत्येतानीमानि
च क्षुद्रमिश्राणीव। बीजानीतराणि चेतराणि चाण्डजानि च
जारुजानि च स्वेदजानि चोद्भिज्जानि चाश्वा गावः
पुरुषा हस्तिनो यत्किंचेदं प्राणि जङ्गमं च पतत्रि च यच्च स्थावरम्।
सर्वं तत्प्रज्ञानेत्रं प्रज्ञाने प्रतिष्ठितं प्रज्ञानेत्रो लोकः प्रज्ञा प्रतिष्ठा
प्रज्ञानं ब्रह्म ॥५.३॥

*Esha brahma esha indra, esha prajaa-patir-ete sarve
devaa imaani cha pancha mahaabhutaani prithivi
vayur-aakaasha aapo jyotimshi-iti-etaani-imaani
cha kshudramishraneeva. Beejaaneetarani
chetaraani cha-andajaani cha jaarujaani cha
svedajaani cha-udbeejajaani cha-ashvaa gaavah
purushaa hastino yat-kimchedam praani jangamam
cha patatri cha yaccha sthavaram sarvam tat-
prajnaanetram prajnaane pratishtitam prajnaanetro
lokah prajnaa pratishtaa prajnaanam brahma. [V.3]*

Chapter Eight

Pure Consciousness Is Brahman

This Brahman, this Indra, this Creator Brahma, all these gods, these five great elements – earth, air, ether, water, fire – all these small creatures, these others, the seeds of creation – the egg-born, the womb-born, sweat-born, sprout-born – horses, cows, men, elephants, whatever else that breathes and moves and flies or is immovable – all these are guided by Consciousness and are supported by Consciousness. The universe has Consciousness for its guide. Consciousness is the basis or stay of all. Verily, Consciousness (Prajnanam) is Brahman; 'Prajnanam-Brahma'.

Aitareya-upanishad [V.3]

Commentary

Consciousness is the ultimate substratum of all things, that in which all things are rooted, in which all things find their very basis. All that we see around us, the sun, the moon, the stars, the five elements – fire, earth, air, water, ether – the fish, the fowl of the air, all beings and creatures that exist in this universe of ours, known and unknown, near and far, all of them ultimately are rooted in Pure Consciousness alone. Consciousness is the giver of their reality, their very existence. Consciousness is the source, support and fulfilment of all existence.

Therefore, says this Upanishad, "*Prajnanam Brahma*", Consciousness is Brahman, the Supreme, the root of all things, the source of all things, the one basis of all things, the eternal, unchanging Reality. Call it Brahman, call it Atman, call it the Supreme Tao, call it Yahweh, call it Allah, or call it Father in Heaven. Call it the ultimate, indescribable state of Nirvana, the 'Great Peace' as Buddha referred to it. Call it the state of perfection, the state of *siddhi*. Call it Ahura Mazda. No matter what you call it, *ek omkar satnaam* – there is but one, unchanging, ultimate Reality which is absolute and non-dual. It is present everywhere as all that exists.

That Great Reality is not something remote, not something inaccessible, not something unapproachable, not something unattainable. It pervades everywhere like the light of the sun pervades this solar system of ours. It indwells all things as their immanent principle just as space is present everywhere. The Vedic religion declares: "All this, whatsoever in this universe that moves or moves not, is indwelt by the Lord." Islam declares: "The Light of Allah dwells in the created human being." Christ said: "The Kingdom of God is within." Judaism teaches: "God created man and breathed His spirit into him."

The breath of God, the spirit of God, dwells in all created beings, especially so in the intelligent creature called man. It dwells in him as that principle which makes this human creature know everything, cognize everything, solve the mystery of all things. This principle of knowing, by which man knows all things, shines at the center of his being – *Prajnanam Brahma*.

It is that by which the eye is able to see and you can recognize form and colour. It is that by which the ear is able to hear and you can distinguish sounds. It is that principle by which you are able to feel and smell. It is that, lacking which, all senses would be as non-existent. By that alone the mind is able to think, the heart is able to feel and the intellect is able to reason, enquire, analyze, discriminate, investigate and move toward knowledge. That principle verily is Brahman.

It shines in the spiritual heart as the primal knowledge. Before you can understand anything, before you can know anything, you first know: "I AM. I exist, therefore I know." The ancient Upanishadic seers said: "Without a knower, knowledge is not possible. The fact that we know something proves beyond the least shadow of a doubt that there is someone who knows." They realized the central, most immediate fact: "I exist and I know that I exist because I am there knowing it." The consciousness of existence is the most immediate and primal manifestation of *Prajna* (Consciousness).

The Upanishad says that, through meditation on this awareness of existence, the sage Vamadeva, after becoming desireless, attained that Absolute Reality which is ageless, deathless, immortal, fearless and omniscient. The sage became merged with the Absolute, even as a river on joining the ocean loses its individuality and becomes the ocean. His sense of individuality and separateness ceased, and he became fully aware of the absence of anything other than his Self.

"Oh, my dear friends," said sage Vamadeva, "Once I had the feeling 'I am the body.' Now, as a result of my *sadhana*, the identity with the body has gone. Now I do not see anything but my Self. I fill all the directions. I pervade all of space. All these gods are non-different from me. I am the four kinds of living beings (those born from earth, from eggs, from sweat and from wombs). From Brahma down to a blade of grass – all are none other than I."

It is to raise your consciousness to that great, sublime height that this most blessed of truths, *Prajnanam Brahma*, has been proclaimed. The most important central truth of the experiences of our great sages is God's all-unifying presence as a common factor present in all His creation, in all His creatures, in everything. This should be pondered in the deep secrecy of your own inner heart.

This should be made the basis of your life and conduct and your day-to-day behaviour with others. Then this type of activity itself will become a spiritual *sadhana* supporting, augmenting, enhancing and enriching your inner spiritual life. Such a *sadhana* has the great power and potential to gradually take you into a state of constant God-awareness. Thus, '*Prajnanam Brahma*' is the great secret revealed in this Upanishad. Pure Consciousness is Brahman; Brahman is Pure Consciousness. This is the truth. One who attains the truth, the truth liberates.

ॐ

Chhandogya-Upanishad
[VI.13.1-3] [VIII.12.1]

लवणमेतदुदके ऽवधायाथ मा प्रातरुप-
सीदथा इति स ह तथा चकार त ँ होवाच
यद्दोषा लवणमुदके ऽवाधा अङ्ग
तदाहरेति तद्धावमृश्य न विवेद ॥६.१३.१॥

Lavanam etat udake avadhaaya atha maa praatarupa-
seedathaa iti sah tathaa chakaara tam hovaacha
ya doshaa lavanam udake avaadhaa anga
tataahara iti tat avamrishya na viveda. [VI.13.1]

यथा विलीनमेवाङ्गास्यान्तादाचामेति
कथमिति लवणमिति मध्यादाचामेति
कथमिति लवणमित्यन्तादाचामेति
कथमिति लवणमित्यभिप्रास्यैतदथ मोपसीदथा
इति तद्ध तथा चकार तच्छश्वत्संवर्तते त ँ होवाचात्र
वाव किल सत्सोम्य न निभालयसेऽत्रैव किलेति ॥६.१३.२॥

Yatha vilinam eva anga asya antaatachama iti
katham iti lavanam iti madhyaatachama iti

katham iti lavanam iti anta tachama iti
katham iti lavanam iti abhipraasya etat atha maa
upasidatha iti tat ha tathaa chakaara tat shashvat
samvartate tam ha uvaacha atra vaava kila sat somya
na nibhaalayase atra eva kileti. [VI.13.2]

स य एषोऽणिमैतदात्म्यमिद्ँ सर्व
तत्सत्य्ँ स आत्मा तत्त्वमसि श्वेतकेतो
इति भूय एव मा भगवान्विज्ञापयत्विति
तथा सोम्येति होवाच॥६.१३.३॥

Sah ya esho-animaa-etad-aatmayam-idam sarvam
tat-satyam sa aatma tat-tvam-asi Svetaketo
iti bhuya eva maa bhagavaan-vijnaapayatu-iti
tathaa somya-iti ha-uvaacha. [VI.13.3]

मघवन्मर्त्यं वा इद्ँ शरीरमात्तं मृत्युना
तदस्यामृतस्याशरीरस्यात्मनोऽधिष्ठानमात्तो
वै सशरीरः प्रियाप्रियाभ्यां न वै सशरीरस्य
सतः प्रयाप्रिययोरपहतिरस्त्यशरीरं वाव सन्तं
न प्रियाप्रियेस्पृशतः ॥८.१२.१॥

Maghavan-martyam vaa idam shareeram-aattam
mrityunaa tadasya amritasya ashreerasya aatamana
adhishthaanam-atta vai sashareerah priyaapriyaa
bhyaam na vai sashareerasya satah priyaapriyoh
apahatihrasti ashareeram vaava santam na
priyaapriye-sprishatah. [VIII.12.1]

Chapter Nine

Connect With and Assert your True Identity

'Place this salt in water and come to me tomorrow morning.' Svetaketu did as he was commanded. In the morning his father said to him, 'Bring me the salt you put into the water last evening.' Svetaketu looked into the water, but could not find it, for it had dissolved. His father then said, 'Please take a sip of it from this side. How is it?' 'It is salt.' 'Taste it from the middle. How is it?' 'It is salt.' 'Taste it from that side. How is it?' 'It is salt.' 'Examine the water as you throw it away and again come to me.' The son did so, saying, 'I cannot see the salt. I only see water.'

His father then said, 'In the same way, O my son, you cannot see the Spirit. But in truth it is here. An invisible and subtle essence is the Atman, the Self of all that exists. That is the Reality; that is the Truth. That Thou Art! – 'Tat Tvam-asi!' ....

Chhandogya-upanishad [VI.13.1-3]

O Indra, please listen to me. It is true that the body is mortal, that it is under the power of death; but it is also the dwelling place of Atman, the Spirit of immortal life. The body, the house of the Spirit, is under the power of pleasure and pain. Anyone who thinks, 'I am the body and the body is myself' can never be free. But when one experiences the joy of the Spirit, the Spirit which is ever free, then that person is free from all bondages related to pleasure and pain.

Chhandogya-upanishad [VIII.12.1]

Commentary

There is one very interesting question to which all of us should find an answer. That question is: This great Reality, this ultimate Truth, this one without a second, this *avinaashi tattva, paraatpara tattva*, (this eternal, indestructible and imperishable Reality) in what way is man related to it? In what way are you, myself and all beings related to it? This is worth knowing.

The answer is as clear as the brilliant sun shining in the midday sky: Know thou, O man! Thou art *not* related to it in any way! Relationship is only when there is duality, when there are two. Only then comes the question of something being related to something else. But in this case, you are yourself That! You are identical with That! You are no other than That! This has to be realized.

Because you are identified with your body and the various senses, you are unable to understand that you are that eternal, effulgent, pure Spirit. You have moved away from your center and have become involved in a state of identity with a non-self, the *anatman*. You have become entangled with some ever-changing, temporary, added factors that limit your consciousness and make you unable to feel your reality in all its glory and grandeur and purity.

Try to clearly perceive this duality. In this lies the key to liberation and blessedness. In this lies the solution to all the problems that you may be experiencing. For practically everything that goes to harass, vex, torment and trouble you is in the part of your being made up of these limiting factors. It is this *deha-adhyaasa* (false identification with the body) that has brought you into this state of bondage, filled with weeping and wailing, but all this is unnecessary and avoidable.

In your real Self, the inner part of your duality, there is no problem, no vexation, no elation or depression, no complication, no trouble of any kind. If one raises his consciousness to this higher dimension and becomes identified with that Supreme Reality, the pairs of opposites cannot touch him. He has no sorrow. He suffers neither heat nor cold, *harsha shoka* (neither joy nor grief), *sukha duhkha* (neither pleasure nor pain). He becomes established in a state of great serenity, which nothing can touch or alter.

The Upanishad is referring to this higher dimension when, in the *maha-vakya* 'Tat Tvam-asi,' it addresses you as "Thou." If you think the term Thou indicates a physical entity, that means you are still identifying yourself with the body, mind and intellect. As long as you are still in that state of consciousness where you are misunderstanding yourself, the Upanishads have failed in their mission.

When the Upanishads say Thou, they are not using ordinary language. They are using neither Sanskrit, English, Hindi nor any other language. They are trying to convey to you a divine experience. They are declaring an experience which is imponderable, beyond the comprehension of the mind or the grasp of the intellect. It is not something based on speculative philosophy, but on the deepest and highest personal realization of our Upanishadic sages.

They are not referring to the seen you, the 'name and form' you. They are referring to the unseen you. They are not referring to anything whatsoever that is seen. They are referring to you as the hidden, unknown seer of all things seen, the knower of all things known. In that dimension, Thou, the hidden seer of all things seen, art That, that which alone prevails. They are referring to your real 'I'.

"I am the Turiya, the unchanging One, calmly witnessing the ever-recurring cycle of waking, dreaming and deep sleep. I am watching. I am experiencing. I am neither awake, nor dreaming, nor in deep sleep, because I have never slept in order to be awake. I am that Awareness that needs no other light to know, for it is the essence of all knowing. It is Knowledge absolute, beginningless and endless. It is the Great Reality, the Truth, Brahman, the Light of lights beyond all darkness. Eternally, I have been what I am. I am that I AM. Wakefulness is my name. Awareness is my name."

This is the real knowledge. This is the meaning that the Upanishad is trying to convey. They say that it is the subtlest of all subtle things. You must make your consciousness attain this subtlety by gradually cleansing and refining it, raising it from its normal physical, psychological level to a spiritual, divine level. Then this heavenly utterance which introduces you to yourself will be grasped and understood.

This is not an ordinary thing. There is the need for years of study and reflection, the need of sitting at the feet of a knower of Brahman and listening to what he has to say about Brahman, about *maya*, about yourself and about the interrelationship of the three, day after day, over months and years. Then you must reflect: "*Guruji* says I am not this gross body and mind. What does he mean? Then, who am I?" You must listen, reflect and meditate. It requires humility and a clear understanding of your real identity, of what this truth is and where you stand. It is not this ordinary thou that is meant. It is something that is inside this thou that is meant when they use the term Thou.

Then, humbly, with patience, diligence and fortitude try to move towards it, and keep on moving, moving, moving. Make your life this slow movement – minute by minute, hour by hour, day after day – never changing direction, never changing your objective, never allowing anything to divert you this way or that from moving toward that center which is your source, the unseen You, and living in and for that great center with every breath and every thought.

This is *sadhana*, this is spiritual life, this is yoga *abhyasa*, this is meditation – dwelling on it, contemplating it. Meditation is every minute, all the twenty-four hours of the day. It is not only when you are alone in your meditation room. Meditation is throughout the day and night, even when you are working or serving or in a crowd. If the meditation stops, your *sadhana* has stopped, your progress has stopped.

Thus, ever strive to connect yourself to that Supreme Reality, to that Light of lights, because, from that to which you connect yourself, its nature will flow into you. An electric bulb is connected to electricity and so it gives you light. But if you sever this connection by turning off the switch, there will be darkness because the electricity is no longer flowing through the bulb.

Link yourself with that pure Spirit. Assert your identity with that Supreme Being who exists as your very Self. And consciously, diligently cultivate this connection and keep on developing it so that it grows and grows and begins to fill your entire consciousness, transforming your sense of personal identity into a higher identity, a divine identity.

"I am part of It. I am no other than It. Within me is shining Its light. Within me, vibrantly alive is that great Spirit. That is what I am. That is my reality. That is the truth of my being. I am a divine principle, a God-principle." Then there comes about a transformation in the inwardness of your hidden subjective awareness.

This is the essence of all *sadhana* and all Vedanta. This is the central *ghoshanaa*, the central declaration of the Upanishads: *You are Divinity! Thou art That! Realize your Self and be free!* Let us claim our birthright and become free souls, not in some post-mortem existence, but in this very life. Living in this body, let us become free souls, *jivanmuktas*, and become forever blessed!

ॐ

Brihadaranyaka-Upanishad
[I.4.9,10]

तदाहुर्यद्ब्रह्मविद्यया सर्वं भविष्यन्तो मनुष्या मन्यन्ते।
किमु तद्ब्रह्मावेद्यस्मात्तत्सर्वमभवदिति॥१.४.९॥

*Tat aahuh yat brahma-vidyayaa sarvam bhavishyanto
manushya manyante; kimu tat-brahmaaved-yasmaat-
tat-sarvam-abhavad-iti.* [I.4.9]

ब्रह्म वा इदमग्र आसीत्तदात्मानमेवावेत्।
अहं ब्रह्मास्मीति । तस्मात्तत्सर्वमभवत्तद्यो
यो देवानां प्रत्यबुध्यत स एव तदभवत्तथर्षीणां
तथा मनुष्याणां तद्धैतत्पश्यन्नृषिर्वामदेवः प्रतिपेदे
अहं मनुरभव ँ सूर्यश्चेति । तदिदमप्येतर्हि य एवं
वेदाहं ब्रह्मास्मीति स इद ँ सर्वं भवति तस्य ह न
देवाश्चनाभूत्या ईशते । आत्मा ह्येषा ँ स भवति
अथ योऽन्यां देवतामुपास्तेऽन्योऽसावन्योऽहमस्मीति
न स वेद यथा पशुरेव ँ स देवानाम् । यथा ह वै

बहवः पशवो मनुष्यं भुञ्ज्युरेवमेकैकः पुरुषो
देवान्भुनक्तयेकस्मिन्नेव पशावादीयमानेऽप्रियं
भवति किमु बहुषु तस्मादेषां तन्न प्रियं यदेतन्मनुष्या
विद्युः ॥१.४.१०॥

*Brahma vaa idamagra aaseet, tat aatmanam evaavet,
aham brahmaasmi-iti; tasmaat-tat-sarvam-abhavat,
tad yo yo devaanaam pratyabudhyata, sa eva tad
abhavat,tatha-rishinaam, tathaa manushyaanaam,
taddhaitat-pashyan-rishir-vama-devah pratipede,
aham manur abhavam suryascha-iti, tat-idam-api
etarhi ya evam veda, aham brahmaasmi-iti, sa idam
sarvam bhavati, tasya ha na devaa cha naabhutya
eeshate,aatmaa hi eshaam sa bhavati, atha yo anyaam
devataam upaaste, anyo'sau anyo'ham asmi-iti, na sa
veda; yathaa pashur, evam sa devaanaam; yathaa ha
vai bahavav pashavo manushyam bhunjyuh , evam-
eka-ekah purusho devaan bhunaktih; ekasminn eva
pashaav adiyamaane'apriyam bhavati, kimu bahushu?
tasmaat eshaam tan na priyam yad etan manushyaa
vidyuh.* [I.4.10]

ॐ

Chapter Ten

Man's Innate Quest for Knowledge and Truth

It has been said that people in ancient times had the knowledge of Brahman and through that knowledge they became the All. What was that knowledge with which they were endowed which enabled them to know the All, become the All, be the All?

Brihadaranyaka-upanishad [I.4.9]

In the beginning, Brahman, the Absolute, alone was. It knew Itself only as "I am Brahman, 'Aham Brahma'smi,' I am the All." Whoever was the individual, celestial or seer who became awakened to this (Knowledge), became the All. This is so even now. Rishi Vamadeva had this knowledge. (Having awakened himself to this Divine Status, to Consciousness of Universal Existence, Vamadeva began to proclaim his experience even while in the womb of his mother.) "I was once the sun, shining in the sky; I was Manu, the progenitor of this world. (Through all these species and forms of existence I have passed to come to this experience.) I am the All."

Even today this is so. Whoever knows thus, 'I am Brahman,' becomes this All. Not even the gods can prevent his becoming thus (attaining this supreme state) because (when one has this Knowledge) he becomes the Self of the gods themselves. So, whoever worships another divinity (other than the universal Self), thinking that he is one and that god another, such a person knows not....

Brihadaranyaka-upanishad [I.4.10]

Commentary

What is the eternal quest of man? There is in-built in man the desire to know. Within the entire creation, this thirst for knowledge is a unique quality that human beings alone possess. All subhuman species are merely engaged in satisfying the needs of the body. Because they do not have a thinking mind, they do not have desires and cravings, ambitions and expectations, schemes and plans for the future. All that a non-human creature wants is enough to eat, some shelter for protection, and the satisfaction of its basic instincts and impulses like procreation. These form the sole quest of subhuman species from the time of birth until they pass away.

Man alone has the potential for a vertical dimension. He wants to know everything. Even an infant, only a few months old, is curious about the world around it. Little children continuously ask, "What is this, what is that?" This quest for knowledge manifests at a very early age, this curiosity, this wanting to know. Ultimately, this thirst for knowledge led man to seek that which alone existed before creation. When that knowledge was gained, something strange happened. What was it? They explain it like this.

There was a doll made of salt living in the interior of the land. Someone told this salt doll, "O dolly, there exists something grand and magnificent called the sea." "What is it?" the doll asked. "It is a vast body of water, so vast and so splendid that it cannot be described." "Is it as big as a well?" inquired the doll. "Oh, no! It is much bigger." "Is it as big as a lake?" "No, no! You can see the circumference of a well or a lake." "Then is it like a river?" "No! Even a river has a further bank that you can see. But this is a body of water so vast that one cannot see its bank." "Oh! Then I must see it!" said the doll.

So it started on a journey. Someone told it, "If you continue to walk in that direction, you will come to the sea." It started walking and kept on walking day and night until, ultimately, it began to feel the sweet, cool breezes arising from the sea and to hear the roar of the waves crashing on the shore.

Finally, it reached the sea and gazed in wonder. For the first time, it could understand, "Ah! Here is a body of water so extraordinarily vast that its other bank cannot be seen!" Then, suddenly, an idea came into the mind of this little doll, "Yes, I cannot see the further shore, but maybe I can see how deep it is. If its distance cannot be known, perhaps I can know its depth. But how can I know it? Well, I must take a plunge and then, when I hit bottom, I will know how deep it is."

So they say, with the desire to know its depth, the doll jumped into the sea. But lo! As it was trying to find the depth, soon, being made of salt, it dissolved in the water and disappeared, and there no longer existed any salt doll to cognize the sea!

Similarly, when our ancient sages wished to know that Brahman which alone existed before creation, they suddenly found that the one who was questing was no more there and Brahman alone was there. They merged into it; they became identified with it. Then they knew with absolute certainty the great truth of the existence of an eternal Being that was All-in-all.

"Sweetness! Sweetness! Sweetness! Everything is sweetness, sweetness beyond description! All is beauty, auspiciousness, bliss!" They were immersed in an ocean of bliss, indescribable bliss. *Anando brahmeti vyajanat*, and they understood that bliss is Brahman. (Taittiriya-upanishad III-6.) They knew that Reality to be present everywhere in all its fullness, always, always unchanging, without contradiction, encompassing everything, pervading everything, indwelling every-thing. That eternal Being was the awareness and con-sciousness of all conscious beings on earth. And they knew themselves to be That alone, the Absolute, the All.

This awareness has been successively borne out by the experience of all the mystics, of all times, of all climes – ancient, medieval, modern, oriental, occiden-tal, everywhere.

The experience which the young Prince Siddhartha had while sitting under the *bodhi*-tree, the experience which changed Siddhartha into a Tathagata, a Buddha, was such an experience. From the top of his head to the tip of his toes, he was filled with bliss! He was intoxicated and inebriated with that bliss to such an extent that he was not aware of the passage of time. He was not aware whether it was night or day. Filled with that bliss, he kept walking to and fro from one side of the garden to the other side in a state of unutterable joy.

For a full forty days he was immersed in that state. For a full forty days he kept walking in that garden, unaware of name or body or time or space, immersed in a peace like no other peace, – a supreme, unalterable, absolute, infinite peace that was not different from God. That state experienced by Lord Buddha is no different from the Satchidananda Brahman, the eternal state of God.

God is peace, God is bliss and God is existence. There is no time when God is not. There is no place where God is not. That peace pervades everywhere just as the air we breathe is everywhere in this whole world. There is not one speck of space where air is not present. If an ordinary thing like air can be all-pervading, what to say of God? There is not a speck of space or an atom of matter where that Peace is not. The entire universe is permeated by that Peace.

What a tremendous realization! What a tremendous realization that at this moment the Bliss of Brahman pervades everywhere within and without! Bliss is the great Reality. Peace supreme, immeasurable, profound Peace, is the great Reality. That Peace, that Bliss, that Fullness, that Light of lights alone exists, and I am

That! *"Aham Brahma'smi!"* In essence, I am no other than That! To ponder this is itself an instant energizer, instant awakener, instant inspirer.

That is the reality, and in this reality we must live. In this truth we must act. With what great strength, elation, positiveness, with what wonderful sublime feelings of zeal we can pursue our spiritual path if we keep ourselves in the awareness of this truth – there is nothing other than Brahman, *ekam eva adviteeyam Brahma.* Brahman alone exists. *Brahmaiva satyam.* This is the ultimate truth.

The greatest philosopher of India, who has been the subject of wonder of many Western philosophers, Jagadguru Sankaracharya said, "That which has been declared in thousands of scriptures I shall tell you in just half a verse: *Shlokardena pravakshyami yaduktam grantha kotibhih; Brahma satyam jagat mithya, jeevo brahmaiva naaparah.* Brahman alone is real, the seen is unreal, and this individual soul is That and That only, no other than That." This is the ultimate truth, the great truth, the one truth.

ॐ

Brihadaranyaka-Upanishad
[V.1.1]

ॐ पूर्णमदः पूर्णमिदं
पूर्णात्पूर्णमुदच्यते।
पूर्णस्य पूर्णमादाय
पूर्णमेवावशिष्यते॥५.१.१॥

Om purnamadah purnamidam
Purnaat-purnamudachyate
Purnasya purnamaadaaya
Purnamev'avashishyate. [V.1.1]

ॐ

Chapter Eleven

The Upanishadic Vision

The great fullness or plenum is Brahman.
What comes from fullness is fullness only.
After the coming out of the effect from
the Cause Supreme,
What remains is ever full.

Brihadaranyaka-upanishad [V.1.1]

Commentary

You are not what you are thinking and dreaming yourself to be. You think yourself to be a petty, little human being, full of weaknesses, full of drawbacks, full of unfortunate limitations, with no other goal than to struggle through life, and sigh and weep. No! No! No! No! All this is a delusion. Snap out of it! This is all due to the wrong knowledge about yourself.

You are *ajo nityah saasvato'yam purnaano na hanyate hanyamaane sareere* – unborn, eternal, permanent, ancient, beyond time, immortal, imperishable and indestructible! (Bhagavad Gita II.20.) You are heir to immortal glory! You are heir to the divine blessedness, which is your original source, a state of divine perfection, which knows no sorrow, no pain, no limitation, no birth and no death. It is a realm of absolute, unalloyed bliss. That is your origin; that is your inalienable permanent state. You exist always in a state of that absolute, indescribable bliss. It is always present. It can never be absent. It is here, now.

Whatever the varying states of the mind, whatever the varying conditions of the body, you are pure bliss. *Ananda* (bliss) is your permanent, unchangeable, natural state, your *sat-avasthaa*, deep within. Delve into that state and then you will discover this wonderful inner splendour. It has been covered over by layers of grosser consciousness due to a false identification with factors that do not constitute your real identity.

You have moved away from your center and identified yourselves with all the things that go to make up the temporary human personality: the five senses of action, the five *pranas*, the five senses of knowledge, and the fourfold inner-instrument of your psychological self. Therefore, in identifying yourself with the non-Self, you have forgotten what you are.

But forgetting what you are does not in any way alter the reality. This fact cannot be changed and that is the truth. Therefore, rejoice! There is no cause for sorrow; there is only a need to correct this error. The message of the Upanishads is: 'Do it NOW! Do not postpone! Make use of the present time to correct this error and attain consciousness of your true reality. Then your life will be nothing but rejoicing, rejoicing, rejoicing!

This servant of the Master is here to call each one of you to awaken from your slumber, from your state of Self-forgetfulness, and begin to live a life of purposeful upward ascent into that spiritual state of *Ananda*-Consciousness which ever exists as your permanent inner essence. May you progress day by day toward this great experience that alone makes every moment of your life a spiritual adventure very worth living!

The practical method for attaining this *sumum bonum* of human life is given in a very concise form in the great scripture Srimad Bhagavad Gita. The Upanishads give you the truth, the great fact of your divinity, of your blissful divine Brahmic nature, and the Gita tells you various ways to attain that state in this very life.

For it is *not* through knowledge and meditation alone that one becomes illumined and liberated. Being and doing count in the spiritual life over and above all knowing. This is why our great illumined sages and seers held before us the twin ideals of *atma-sakshatkara*, direct realization of the Self, and *paropakara*, selfless service to all beings and creatures in God's creation.

Erudition is admirable. A great deal of learning and knowledge is not bad. But certainly one must see that it is not enough. You may read all the philosophical books and you may be able to sit for hours in *dhyana*, but if your heart is not filled with love, kindness and compassion for others, you may obtain everything, but to obtain illumination and liberation will not be possible. To do even a little is the essence of the spiritual life. Hinting at this in the latter half of the twelfth chapter of the Bhagavad Gita, Lord Krishna tells us who is dear to Him.

The great Lord Buddha, at the time of his departure, calls all of his disciples together and tells them that now the *Tathagata* will be entering into *pari-nirvana* and this will be his last teaching unto all. He says: "O *bhikkshus*, do not neglect your own highest welfare. Do not neglect your own highest good. In your life, be a light unto yourself and be a lamp unto the feet of others. Go forth and traverse the highways and byways of this great land for the welfare of the many and the happiness of the many."

This is the central ideal placed before you to live for and to die for. Ever be a channel for the expression of God's perfection, God's love, compassion, kindness and consideration. Feel for others; identify with the joy and sorrow of others. In the presence of sorrow, immediately act to be an angel of mercy, peace and joy. Make yourself a center of all that is godly, all that is beautiful, sublime and divine.

Choose always to manifest the truth that is within you, and never anything else but this. Choose to be what you really are. In this choice lies not only your own highest good, but the good of all beings and creatures. In this choice lies the highest well-being of the contemporary world in which you live. This is the one thing needful. In this fertile field of spiritualized living, *jnana* and *dhyana* will bear the fruit of illumination. Not otherwise.

Reflect well upon these great truths which are our inheritance from the great sages of our radiant past. They are not to be neglected, not to be taken lightly. These truths are to be deeply pondered and earnestly applied in our daily life, at each step, every moment, always. Then they will become truths that liberate us, truths that transform us, truths that make our *sadhana* fruitful in God-experience. There is no doubt about it.

May God bless you! May the saints and sages of the Upanishads inspire you with the determination to attain the goal in this very life and not postpone it one second further! Therefore, let me once again re-echo the great call of the Upanishads! *"Uttishthata jaagrata praapya varaan nibodhata!* Arise! Awake! Having reached the great teachers, realize the Truth!"

When you awake each morning at the dawn of a new day, remember that you are an immortal soul. Remember that this life has been given to you to attain that supreme experience. With this new vision, move forward from today into all the tomorrows that go to make up your life until you become established forever in the state of supreme bliss, perfection, blessedness and liberation. God bless you.

Om Shantih, Shantih, Shantih.
Om Peace, Peace, Peace.

*Then the sage said to the disciples: "This much alone
I know of this Highest Brahman. There is nothing
higher than this."*

*Bowing to him in adoration, the disciples said:
"You are in truth our Father who has saved us from
ignorance and has led us to the Further Shore.*

*Glory to the supreme Rishis!
Glory to the supreme Seers!"*

Prasna Upanishad [VI.7-8]

Tadvaktaaramavatu.

Om Shantih, Shantih, Shantih.

Om Tat Sat

Glossary

abhyasa: repetition, practice.

advaita: non-duality, monism.

ananda: bliss, happiness, joy.

anandamaya kosha: blissful sheath or *karana sarira*, the seed body which contains the *mula ajnana* or the potentialities.

anatma(n): the not-Self.

annamaya-kosha: food-sheath; gross physical body.

aparoksha'nubhuti: direct perception of the Truth.

ashtanga yoga: yoga with eight limbs; *raja yoga* of Patanjali Maharshi.

Atma(n): the Self.

atma-nivedanam: dedicating one's entire self to the divine; self-surrender.

atma-satshatkara: Self-realization.

avasthaa: state.

avatara: incarnation of the Divine.

Bhagavad Gita: 700 verses from the great Hindu epic Mahabharata recording the Discourse between Lord Krishna and Arjuna on the battlefield of Kurukshetra, prior to the commencement of the great war and giving in clear and concise form the highest teachings and truths.

Bhagavan: the Lord.

Bharatavarsha: India; derived from the name of the famous, ancient King Bharat.

bhakti: devotion; love (of God).

bhakti-yoga: path of devotion.

bhav(a): mental attitude, feeling, purity of thoughts.

bhikkshu: monk, mendicant, sannyasin.

brahma-jnana: direct knowledge of Brahman.

Brahman: the Absolute Reality, Existence-Consciousness-Bliss-Absolute. *brahmanistha*: ever established in Brahman.

brahma-vidya: science of Brahman, knowledge of Brahman.

chidananda: Consciousness-Bliss.

chidghana: mass of Consciousness.

chinmaya: full of Consciousness.

chit: absolute consciousness or intelligence.

chitsvaroopa: of the very form of consciousness.

deha-adhyaasa: false identification with the body.

dharma: righteous way of living as enjoined by the Vedas; properties, duty.

dhyana: meditation.

duhkha: pain, misery, sorrow, grief.

guru: teacher, spiritual preceptor.

harsha: exhilaration, joy.

japa: repetition of God's Name again and again; repetition of a mantra.

jivanmukta: one who is liberated in this life.

jnana jyoti: effulgent wisdom awareness.

jnana yoga: the path of spiritual knowledge.

jnana: spiritual knowledge, wisdom of the Reality or Brahman.

jnana-kanda: the section of the Vedas dealing mainly with the eternal verities or the Absolute Truth; the Upanishads dealing with the Param Brahman (the Supreme Absolute, the transcendental Reality).

jyotih: illumination; luminosity; effulgence.

kalaa: part, ray.

karma: action. It is of three kinds: *sanchita* (all the accumulated actions of all previous births), *prarabdha* (the particular portion of such karma allotted for being worked out in the present life), and *agami* (current karma being freshly performed by the individual); it is the karma operating through the law of cause and effect binding the *jiva* or the individual soul to the wheel of birth and death.

karmendriya: organ of action: tongue (speech), hands, feet, genital and anus are the organs of action.

kosha: sheath; bag; scabbard; a sheath enclosing the soul; there are five such concentric sheaths or chambers one above the other, namely, the sheaths of bliss, intellect, mind, life-force and the gross body.

maha-vakya: (lit.) great sentence; Upanishadic declarations, four in number, expressing the highest Vedantic truths or the identity between the individual soul and the Supreme Soul; they are: 1) *prajnanam brahma* (Consciousness is Brahman) in the Aitareya Upanishad of the Rig Veda; 2) *Aham Brahmasmi* (I am Brahman) – in Brihadaranyaka Upanishad of the Yajur-Veda; 3) *Tat Tvam-asi* (That Thou art) – in the Chhandogya Upanishad of the Sama Veda; 4) *Ayam Atma Brahma* (This Self is Brahman) – in the Mandukya Upanishad of the Atharva Veda.

manana: constant thinking; reflection; meditation on the eternal verities; the second of the three steps on the path of knowledge.

manomaya kosha: one of the sheaths of the Self, consisting of the mind.

mantra: sacred syllable or word or set of words through the repetition and reflection of which one attains perfection or realization of the Self.

maya: the illusive power of Brahman; the veiling and the projecting power of the universe.

namana: worship, bowing, paying respect.

nididhyasana: profound and deep meditation; third step in Vedantic *sadhana*, after 'hearing' and 'reflection'.

paramananda: supreme bliss.

Paramatma: the Supreme Self.

param-brahma: the Supreme Absolute, the transcendental Reality.

paropakara: the good and welfare of others; service of others.

prana: vital energy; life-breath; life-force.

pranamaya kosha: one of the sheaths, consisting of the *pranas* and the five *karmendriyas*.

prarabdha-karma: the particular portion of one's total karma allotted for being worked out in the present life

purusha: the Supreme Being; the Self that abides in the hearts of all things.

raja-yoga: the royal yoga of meditation; the system of yoga generally taken to be the one propounded by Patanjali Maharshi, i.e., *ashtanga yoga*.

rishi: sage; seer of the Truth.

sadhana: spiritual practice.

samsara: worldly existence; phenomenal appearance; transmigration.

sanatana: eternal, everlasting.

sanatana dharma: the eternal Truth.

sanatana vaidika dharma: the ancient path of Righteousness and Truth.

sannyasa: renunciation of social ties; the last stage of Hindu life, viz., the stage of spiritual meditation.

sat: Existence Absolute, Being, Reality, Truth.

satchidananda: Existence-Consciousness-Bliss Absolute.

satshatkara: direct realization; experience of Absoluteness; Brahmajnana.

shloka: a Sanskrit verse.

shoka: grief.

siddhanta: the established doctrine.

sravana: hearing of the *srutis* or scriptures; ear.

srutis: the Vedas; the revealed scriptures of the Hindus; that which has been heard; ear.

sukha: pleasure, happiness, joy.

svabhava: one's own nature or potentiality; innate nature.

svaroopa: essence, essential nature, the essential nature of the Self, Reality, *satchidananda*, the true nature of being.

turiya: superconscious state; the noumenal Self of creatures which transcends all conditions and states.

Upanishad: Knowledge portion of the Vedas; texts dealing with the ultimate truth and its realization.

Veda: the most ancient authentic scripture of the Hindus; a revealed scripture and therefore free from imperfection; the word 'Veda' comes from the root 'vid', 'to know'; it means a book of wisdom; the ideas contained in the Vedas are eternal and God-given.

Vedanta: the end portion of the Vedas (lit.), the Upanishads.

vichar(a): inquiry into the nature of the Self, Brahman, Truth Absolute.

vijnanamaya kosha: the sheath of the intellect or *buddhi*, which gives a sense of knowledge.

yoga: (lit.) union; abstract meditation or union with the Supreme Being; the name of the philosophy by the sage Patanjali, teaching the process of union of the individual with the Universal Soul; union with God; any course that makes for such union; unruffled state of mind under all conditions; yoga is mainly of four types: *karma, bhakti, raja and jnana*.